DELPHOS PUBLIC LIBRARY
309 West Second Street
Delphos, Ohio 45833-1695

Celebrating

Easter

By: Shelly Nielsen
Illustrated by: Marie-Claude Monchaux

E
Nie

942849

Published by Abdo & Daughters, 6535 Cecilia Circle, Edina, Minnesota 55439.

Library bound edition distributed by Rockbottom Books, Pentagon Tower, P.O. Box 36036, Minneapolis, Minnesota 55435.

Copyright © 1992 by Abdo Consulting Group, Inc., Pentagon Tower, P.O. Box 36036, Minneapolis, Minnesota 55435. International copyrights reserved in all countries. No part of this book may be reproduced in any form without written permission from the publisher. Printed in the United States.

Edited by: Rosemary Wallner

LIBRARY OF CONGRESS CATALOGING-IN-PUBLICATION DATA

Nielsen, Shelly, 1958-
    Easter / written by Shelly Nielsen; [edited by Rosemary Wallner]
    p. cm. -- (Holiday celebrations)
    Summary: Rhyming text introduces aspects of this important Christian holiday.
    ISBN 1-56239-069-4
    1. Easter--Juvenile literature. [1. Easter.] I. Wallner, Rosemary, 1964- II. Title. III. Series: Nielsen, Shelly, 1958- Holiday celebrations.
GT4935.N54   1992   394.2'683283--dc20   91-73032

International Standard Book Number:	Library of Congress Catalog Card Number:
1-56239-069-4	91-73032

Celebrating

Easter

marie-claude monchaux

Here Comes Spring!

Breathe deep . . .
Take a peek . . .
Spring came
while we were asleep!
Tulips lift their petal heads,
while rain tickles the
flower beds.
Easter and spring
must be best friends;
they arrive together
when winter ends.

Egg Art

Boil some eggs;
bring art supplies;
I'll make Easter eggs
to dazzle your eyes.
Spread out the paper;
spray on the glue;
add a sprinkle of glitter,
first yellow . . .
then blue.
Ta-da! All done.
What do you think?
For my very next trick,
I'll make eggs purple and pink.

Spring Baby

Cottonball bunny
kick up your heels;
after shivery-cold winter
how *good* running feels.
The yard is sprouting
with flowers for smelling,
and grass that tickles
your furry belly.
It's a wonderful world —
and I ought to know.
I was a spring baby, too,
once —
long ago.

Flowers for You

I picked a bouquet
to put in a vase,
and brought a smile
to Mama's face.
A beautiful smell
filled the room;
Easter flowers
must wear perfume.

Where Does Candy Come From?

My little brother, Rodney, is actually kind of funny.
He thinks that chocolate eggs are dropped
by chocolate Easter bunnies.
He tells me that jelly beans are laid
by hens on rainbow farms,
and marshmallow chicks are the candy babies
of big marshmallow moms.

Hello, Butterfly

Butterfly, flap.
  Butterfly, soar.
Decorate Easter
in white, blue, and orange.

Butterfly, sail
  as high as you dare;
Flutter like a flower
  in the spring air.

Make-a-Basket

Won't Brianna love it?
Won't Brianna squeal
when she sees the Easter basket
made just for her by me?

The inside's lined with plastic,
and filled with garden dirt.
I sprinkled in some grass seeds
and watered it (just a squirt).

I waited . . . and watched . . . and waited . . .
and set it in the sun.
And then — know what? —
the blades came up;
they sprouted one by one.

On Easter, I'll add some candies
and a satin bow.
I bet Brianna will love it.
I would — wouldn't you?

Show Time

In the Easter show,
I play a yellow chick.
When the curtains open,
I say, "cheep, cheep, cheep!"
I'm glad I'm not a rabbit
who doesn't make a sound,
he just hippity-hops
around.

Hunt for Treasures

Dash, run, squeal, and shout . . .
find Easter eggs hidden about.
Here's a striped one under the tree
half green, half yellow . . .
where could the other ones be?
Aha! Here's a pink one in the bird bath,
and another one beside a watering can.
When it comes to egg hunts
there's no escape.
I know every egg's hiding place.

Crack-Crack-Crack

Grab an Easter egg
and give it a tap.
Watch the eggshell
crack-crack-crack.
Roll it on a table,
peel it for your snack.
Then gobble it down
— simple as that!

Easter Outfit

Dad has the camera
to take a shot
of my Easter outfit
and me — all dressed up.
"Hold still," he calls,
"and stand up straight;
say 'cheese,' please,
and *wait*."
I'm grinning like crazy,
but I itch from scratchy lace;
there's a hair in my mouth,
and a tickle on my face.
While Dad focuses the camera,
I'll scratch double quick.
But as soon as I reach —
                    "Click!"

All Set to Share

Help set the table for an Easter feast.
Let's see . . . there's ten of us, at least:
a place for Aunt Sue and Uncle Harry,
our cousins, Carolyn and Barry,
Grandpa and Grandma,
Mom and Dad, too.
That leaves me and you.
Whew!
Mom says Easter's fun to share . . .
Know what?
It's true!

Easter Feast

Help yourself to mashed potatoes,
hot cross buns, ham, tomatoes,
salad, beans, asparagus . . .
How long can this Easter feast last?
We're coming to the final part —
whipping cream on cherry tarts.
We've scraped our plates
and cleaned each bowl,
so we push back our chairs and groan,
"We're full!"

Last Game

Night's coming; light is fading;
my cousins and I keep right on playing.
We chase and holler and tag each other
(we even include my little brother).
Playing with cousins is fun at Easter.
I'm glad it comes once a year, at least.

DELPHOS PUBLIC LIB

2601 9100 020 983 0

DISCARDED